917.1   Kurelek, William
Kur

     Prairie boy's
     winter

A PRAIRIE BOY'S WINTER

A PRAIRIE BOY'S WINTER

Paintings and Story by William Kurelek

1973

HOUGHTON MIFFLIN COMPANY BOSTON

Library of Congress Cataloging in Publication Data

Kurelek, William, 1927-
  A prairie boy's winter.

  SUMMARY: Text and twenty color paintings depict
the rigors and simple pleasures of the winter on the
prairies during the stark 1930's.
  1. Children in Canada--Juvenile literature.
2. Winter in art--Juvenile literature. (1. Farm
life. 2. Winter. 3. Great Plains) I. Title.
F1021.5.K87   917.1'03'60222   73-8913
ISBN 0-395-17708-1

H 10 9 8 7 6 5 4

A *Prairie Boy's Winter* is published simultaneously in
the United States by Houghton Mifflin Company of Boston
and in Canada by Tundra Books of Montreal.

For everyone who ever spent a winter on the prairies
— and for all the others who wonder what it was like

A PRAIRIE BOY'S WINTER

1. Crows Leaving Before Winter

It was chilly. The skies hung heavy and gray as William, his brother,
John, and his sister, Winnie, joined other children on the highway, schoolbound.

The crows had been loitering around in great flocks, quarreling, cawing,
and raiding farmers' cornfields. Now they were finally leaving. They flew south
every fall about this time to escape the harsh prairie winter. In the cow
pasture the leaves had fallen from the white poplars and the oaks, leaving the
crows' nests bare in the high branches.

It would be five months before one of those noisy black birds came flapping
back over the pasture bush to announce the end of winter.

2. The First Snowfall

William behaved like children all over the world at the first snowfall.
He became giddy with excitement and held his mouth open to
catch the first big juicy flakes spiraling slowly downward.

Immediately after school, William and Winnie were sent by their mother to
fetch the cows. For the past few days the animals had been huddling
under the straw pile to keep warm. From now until spring they would
remain in the barn, apart from a brief daily visit to the water trough.

This year William's father had managed to lay up plenty of cattle feed for the
winter. Two large clover stacks had been built beside the warmer south
side of the barn, and a silo hole had been filled with ensilage and
covered over. Ensilage is finely chopped green corn that has partly fermented
under its own weight. Cows go crazy over their daily ration of it —
one forkful per cow — just as cats do over catnip. But their main dinner
was hay, and some of that was already in the hayloft.

3. Calling Pigs to Feed

The first snowfall was heavy and the next day the sun shone on a dazzling white, cold landscape.

William helped his mother carry feed to the pigpen. While she poured it into the trough, he counted the pigs as they came out of the straw. His mother called, "Tsyok, tsyok, tsyok, tsyow," which the pigs understood as, "Food's on!" The pail had to be empty before the first pig reached the trough, because pigs are so greedy and bad-mannered they climb into the trough with all four feet. Then you couldn't put any more feed in unless you poured it over their heads.

Bad as their table manners are, pigs do keep their living quarters clean, contrary to what most people believe. William, John, and Winnie saw this for themselves later when the pigs had been hauled away to market. The cave in the middle of the straw stack that they reached by a tunnel, was cozy and perfectly clean. In summer, the pigpen was overgrown with weeds so tall the children couldn't even see each other over the tops. But in winter, the dried-up stalks of the weeds could be broken off and used as spears in tribal warfare.

4. Fox and Geese

The games of farm children were handed down from generation to generation.
One of them was always played at school after the first snowfall. By
shuffling their feet, the children traced a large pie-shaped design in the snow, clear
down to the dried-up brown grass. William and his friends called an eight-
piece pie Fox and Geese, and a four-piece pie Cat and Mice. Usually these pies, or
wheels with spokes, were tramped out in a clear unspoiled stretch of snow just
outside the schoolyard which the children had to crawl through the school fence to reach.

The game was already in full swing. William snagged his jacket on the barbed wire
in his rush to join. A fox had been chosen — or had volunteered — and he chased
anyone he thought he could tag. The tagged one would then become the fox.

It was no fun being a fox if you were slow, because you got teased a lot. "Nyah! Nyah!
Can't catch me!" Of course, everyone, fox and goose, had to stay on the lines of
the wheel or pie, and it was hard to pass anyone without falling into the snow and
being disqualified. Some tried to sneak up as close as possible to the fox and then
escape him narrowly. Others made faces at him from the safety of home. Home was
the hub of the wheel, and there the geese were safe.

5. Rink Making

William didn't really like hockey or any other rough sport because he wasn't strong, athletic, or quick. But when the time came to make a hockey rink, the hockey lovers persuaded everyone to pitch in and help.

The work could not begin until the ground was frozen hard under the snow. Then an area was marked out between the school barn and the pump, and the snow was cleared right down to the grass. It was pushed or shoveled to the sides to make a shallow bank around the rink. Then, using all the pails that could be gathered together and the old copper boiler off the school stove, the children flooded the rink with water beginning at the corner farthest from the pump. The water steamed up for only a few minutes before the cold of the ground and the air gripped it solid.

By using both recesses and the noon hour, they could get the first shell of ice laid in one day but it would be very bumpy. The rink had to be reflooded at least once a week to keep the bumps covered, and, of course, it had to be cleared after every snowfall.

6. Hockey Hassles

William dreaded arguments, and there always seemed to be arguments in hockey games. A common cause was the lack of a net. For goal posts, two oak poles had been driven into the ground before flooding, but without a net it was often difficult to tell which side of the post the puck had gone. William was a poor skater and preferred not to play on skates, so he was made goalie. This put him right in the center of the arguments. All the boys joined in. Sometimes, one side pretended to be generous and give in on a goal. But usually the side that shouted the loudest and longest won the point.

William made his own shin pads by cutting off old trouser legs and sewing them up and down at regular, spaced intervals. Into these narrow pockets he slipped thin slats from apple boxes and then attached the pads to his legs with rubber sealing rings from his mother's preserve jars.

The goalie's stick was easier to make than those of the offensive players. William had only to nail two layers of support slats on the side of a board. But other boys spent days examining branches and small trees on their way home from school in the hope of finding one suitable for a hockey stick. Some simply nailed two thin boards together neatly at the right angle, and hoped they would not come apart at a crucial moment during the game. A lucky few got real hockey sticks for Christmas. Jesse, the star player, was among the lucky and it was often he who argued with William over which side of the post the puck went.

7. Will He or Won't He?

On the frozen sea of snow that stretched across farmlands broken only by barbed-wire fences, prairie boys would find jack-rabbit trails. And their eyes lit up: "Game!"

William and John could not afford bullets for their father's .22 rifle. Even if they could have, the walk knee-deep in bush snow and the long, cold lying-in-wait were very difficult. Nor was it easy to spot a rabbit in the first place because of his white winter coat. So what was simpler than to set a snare?

On nights when the traps were out, William would lie awake in bed imagining the next unsuspecting rabbit loping down the trail in the lonely winter stillness under the Northern Lights. "Will he or won't he get caught?" he wondered. What a thrill it was for him and John in the morning as they inspected their little "trap line" to find a frozen rabbit here, another there. Frozen, unskinned rabbits sold for twenty-five cents; four rabbits fetched a dollar, a fantastic sum for an eleven- or twelve-year-old boy in those hard years.

8. Hauling Hay

No matter how much hay was laid up in the barn, there was never enough to last the winter.

William liked the drive across the frozen fields to the hay stacks, but not the work after he arrived there. The stack usually had a cap of snow packed into it by the wind and glazed hard by the sun of warmer winter days. The cap had to be broken with fork or shovel and stripped off; otherwise one would be forever tugging at strands of hay rooted deep in the snow and ice.

William had built many of the stacks himself in the summer, and he had learned that it didn't pay to do the work carelessly. If the stacks were not made properly, rain would seep in and cause moldy patches — and bring a scolding from his father.

The horses cooled off during the loading. Icicles were hanging from their nostrils by the time the last pitchfork was stuck into the crown of the load and William's father took the reins and called out, "Giddap!" He and William turned their collars up and wrapped the horse blanket around themselves, for the heat and sweat worked up during the loading could bring on a chill if they were not well covered. Hoarfrost coated their eyebrows as they set out on the slow wobbly ride homeward.

9. Skiing Behind the Hayrack

Sometimes the children turned the job of hauling hay into a sport. Where William first got the idea of several people skiing side by side behind the hay wagon he could not tell you. There were no lakes near their prairie farm and he had never seen water-skiers. But one day he attached a long piece of hay wire to the back of his father's rack with a stick at the other end to hold on to. As the rack headed down the road, going at a trot pace because it was still empty, it pulled him along too, at wire's length. Winnie and John then joined in with their tow wires. Sliding behind the hayrack, the skiers discovered that their speed increased simply by pointing their skis off to the side of the road. Extra danger and thrills could be got by actually skiing right onto the roadside fields. They crossed the barbed-wire fence on the back of a high snowdrift, and hoped that another big drift farther along would allow them a chance to get back onto the road.

William tried carving his first skis out of boards, but he could never get enough curl-up at the front and they caused tumbles at the slightest snag. Finally, the three children persuaded their parents to buy them the cheap willow skis they had seen advertised in the mail-order catalogue. The binding was the simplest kind: a single strap passing through a flat hole in the middle of the ski. It was usually at the hole that the skis finally broke, but not before they had given a lot of pleasure.

10. Watering Cows in Winter

Before William's father made a pipeline from the pump house to the barn and installed water troughs in the mangers, the dairy herd had to be watered at an outside trough. Even when it was snowing and blowing, the cows had to go out, for eating dry hay and chop for twenty-four hours made them very thirsty. Because it was such an ordeal for both man and beast, the chore was limited to once a day, and the children had to help.

John would undo the stanchions in late afternoon and chase the whole herd into the bitter cold outside. The cows would hunch up their backs and charge toward the water trough to get the whole experience over with as quickly as possible. William, dressed in his warmest red mackinaw, worked the trough, hacking away at the crust of ice formed the day before. Meanwhile, his mother thawed out the pump with a kettle of hot water so that fresh water could be pumped in. She tried not to pump more water than the cows would drink, for any that was left would freeze solid and only have to be chopped out the next day. The water was so cold that now and then as the cows drank they had to lift their teeth out of it when the chill became too painful.

11. Chasing a Chicken in the Snow

Another chore that the children helped with was cleaning chicken manure out of the coop. This was easy work compared to barn cleaning, for chicken droppings were light and much mixed with straw. Usually a fresh sunny day was chosen for the job.

Chickens are jumpy. If anyone cleaning under them makes an unexpected move, the whole flock will fly into the air. One chicken might even fly out the door to the glistening snow. Then, William's mother would yell, "William! Winnie! Come here, catch the one that got away!" Now, there is nothing so stupid as a chicken. You can't drive it, for it does not follow a straight course away from humans, as cows or horses or geese do. Nor will it let itself be caught. The best you can do, as William found out from experience, is to keep the chicken moving until it is worn out. Then you hedge in, and pounce! If you're lucky, you can grab it by the leg and carry it squawking back into the coop.

12. Skating on the Bog Ditch

Although William didn't care for hockey or rink skating, he did like skating on
the bog because it appealed to his exploring instinct. In deep winter the
excitement was in finding out how many miles up the main drainage ditch the
skaters could go before they were stopped by snowdrifts across the ice. In
the early spring, whole miles of the bog were covered with water that froze during
the night; the next morning a skater had an immense feeling of freedom as
he cruised down the expanse.

Sometimes the water near the great spring would be too warm to allow the ditch to
freeze solid; these weak spots stopped the skaters. William took tumbles
when his skate got caught in reeds. Once, a friend of Winnie's broke through and
got wet up to her middle. She walked all the way home with her clothes
frozen like a suit of armor.

13. Hauling Firewood

Hauling firewood was one chore that William never got to like. He could carry the wood by armfuls to the house from the woodpile, but that meant too much trudging through the snow. Better to load up a sleigh, and if John and Winnie would push or pull, that made it easier.

If for some reason the whole house had to be warmed, a full wagonload of wood had to be thrown in through the cellar window. The octopuslike furnace gobbled up the poplar logs like twigs, so, usually, most of the house was left unheated.

William didn't venture into the cold rooms except when really necessary. Going to bed was one such necessity. He would run up the stairs, strip quickly to his longjohn underwear, and dive under the blankets. Making a tight curl-up cubbyhole for himself, he would breathe and breathe until his hot breath made it tolerably warm.

The kitchen, though, had to be heated without fail, for the stove fire cooked the meals, dried the snow-wet clothing, and melted snow to make soft water for the laundry. So hauling wood was a regular chore. If the woodpile was snowed in, William had to dig for the logs. Sometimes, on the way to the front door, Winnie drew the sleigh over a deep rut and the load would start to slip. Iron bars held the wood at the two ends, but they didn't stop it from slipping out the sides. "Whoa! Whoa!" he would yell, as was the habit of farm children playing Horse and Wagon.

14. The Blizzard

There was at least one blizzard every winter, and this winter it came unexpectedly. Shortly after four o'clock, as William was returning from school, it began to snow. At first it looked like an ordinary snowfall, but by the time he had done his barn chores, it was snowing more heavily and a wind had started up. "Maybe," Winnie said wistfully, "we'll not have to go to school tomorrow." At bedtime William heard the wind shrieking around his bedroom window, but he could see nothing, for the window was frosted over.

The next morning, all the outside was a howling whiteness that took his breath away when he stepped out. There would be no school for sure, because children had been known to lose their way and freeze to death in such a blizzard. Farmyard chores were kept to a minimum, but some had to be done. William raised his mackinaw collar as high as possible, shielded his face with his hand, and plunged through the snow to the chicken coop to gather eggs and give the chickens water.

Most of the time the children stayed in the house looking out now and then through a melted patch on the pane of the kitchen window. By the end of the second day they could contain themselves no longer. They dressed extra warmly and ventured out into the storm to examine the half-dozen places in and around the farmyard where the wind had sculpted extra-high drifts.

15. Sundogs and Sticky Iron

The big blizzard that came each winter was followed by an eerie silence. It was partly an illusion, a contrast to the howling fury the ear had got used to after three days and nights. The wind had stopped and the sun was dazzling over the crisp, fresh, white landscape. In the clear air the train running three miles to the west of the farm sounded as if it were chugging down the highway, just up the lane.

As William went out on an errand, he noticed another odd thing. The sun had two little snippets of rainbow some distance away from it, just above the horizon. His father referred to this in Ukrainian: "The sun has ears," he said. But the other children in school with William knew they were called sundogs.

The double tree of the winter sleigh was broken, so William had to fetch one off a summer wagon. He waded through snow and tried to lift the bolt that held it to the wagon tongue, but his thick mitts were too clumsy. Forgetfully, he slipped one off and grabbed the bolt with his fingers. "Yayk!" he gasped. His fingers had stuck to the metal and it burned like fire. He shook it and shook it. Finally, it came off without tearing his skin. That was a 40°-below-zero lesson he did not forget that winter!

16. Snowdrift Fun

Back at school after the blizzard, the children could hardly wait until recess to explore the drifts. The biggest ones were against the bush to the northwest of the schoolyard. The wind had swept the snow there from across two miles of open fields. The bush broke the force of the wind and the snow settled in its twigs and branches, where it lay loosely packed. On the drift's surface the snow was packed and glazed, but once you broke through that upper crust, either by shoveling or jumping up and down on it, the rest of the way was easygoing.

The drifts were so high the children could make two-story apartments by honeycombing the snow with tunnels and caves. If they came in from the top they kept kicking their feet downward and then southward until they emerged into the open on the face of the drifts. At the elbow of the tunnel William and his companions carved out a meeting room for both girls and boys. Bright sunlight, reflecting off the tunnel walls, even lit the chamber dimly. So happily absorbed were the pupils in their building that they didn't hear the small school bell. The teacher had to use the big bonger up in the belfry to get them to return, cheeks glowing, to their desks. Their outer clothes, packed with snow in every crease, were left to dry by the boxstove in the corner.

17. Milk Truck on Snowplowed Road

Following the big blow, the road to the town five miles away was plugged
solid with drifts that reached as high as the telephone wires. Milk had to be got to
the city, and everyone — the farmer, the creamery, the trucker — wanted
it to get there.

Eventually, a snowplow would batter its way through the east-west line, pushing
enormous banks of snow to left and right. It had extra wing-type snow
scrapes to push the tops of the furrows farther away, so they would not slide down
and fill up the road again.

The newly cleared road looked like an open tunnel with room for just one
vehicle to pass through it. Saturday morning, as William went to town with his
father in their sleigh wagon, they met the milk truck coming toward them.
The driver gunned his motor, sending clouds of powdered snow billowing up behind
him, as he rushed to beat them to the crossroads and turn into a dairy farm
so they could get by.

A week later another, smaller, snowstorm filled the road to the top once more,
and the snowplow gave up. The farmers then had to haul their milk by
horse and sleigh over the tops of the drifts to meet the milk truck at the main
highway.

18. Snowball Weather

There was something different about the snow on balmy late winter days:
it was no longer powdery. Then, not even hockey could hold the attention of
William's schoolmates. Everyone wanted to make snowballs. Sometimes
a snowman was made, but that was thought to be kids' stuff. Competition and
marksmanship were the thing. The children threw as far as possible to
knock each other's hats off, or they organized sides — if anything that came so
naturally can be called organization — for a snowball war.

Sometimes forts were built first. A small mound of snow was made and
rolled across the yard. It picked up the sticky snow under its weight and got
fatter and fatter, until in time at least three people were needed to push it.
That would be big enough! By then it had to be on location.

As a rest from pushing, William knelt and made ammunition. Snowballs were
made most easily and firmly with bare hands. When his hands got too
cold, he would put his flopping wet mitts on again and return to pushing the rest
of the fort together.

In the war that followed, collars and scarves were loosened, caps came off,
and mitts were lost. The children were all very wet and panting when they went
back into the school after lunch.

19. Testing Depth of Spring Run-off

Spring was on its way when most of the snow had gone from the schoolyard and the little that remained lay in drifts along the fences. The ice on the rink became too "rubbery" for skating, but the hockey enthusiasts played on in their boots. It was a time of year when William liked to go off by himself to explore the water holes. He was fascinated by spring run-off water. He never knew from day to day how deep it was, so he had to test it — just as mountains have to be climbed.

Testing was risky, but that was part of the thrill. Ice or snow beneath the surface of the water might suddenly give, and then he had a rubber boot full of icy cold water. Out he would scramble, for even one dry foot was better than none. He emptied the boot, tugged off the soaking sock, and wrung it out. The trouser leg could be wrung a little against the leg, or slipped down over the outside of the boot.

William had early experiences of wettings — against his will. Older boys would bully the youngest during recess to test the spring ice on the ditch in front of the school. They would break through, of course, and the teacher would have to dry out their clothes behind the school stove. Now that William was growing older, he remembered — and got no one wet except sometimes himself.

20. Return of the First Crow

Melting snow and ice were proof that winter was over, but William really
dated spring from an event that occurred a month earlier. It is said that the robin
is the first sign of spring. But on the prairies many say it's the prairie
horned lark, a small cousin of the meadow lark, that heralds spring. At the very
first thaw, these larks can be seen, sometimes in twos and threes, standing
beside puddles in the field. For William, however, there was something special
about the crow — perhaps because of its very noisy, very noticeable departure
at the beginning of winter — that made its return spell *spring* for him. Maybe too,
it was because the crow is a large bird, and black, so it stood out against the snow.

Crows came back singly, or in pairs, about the end of March. It was then
they were sighted by the children on their way to or from school. The lucky first-
sighters threw up their hands, and even their caps, in exultation, chanting,
"I saw it! I saw it! I saw the first crow! Spring's here!"

William Kurelek grew up on the prairies during the hard 1930s.
The first several years of his life were lived on a grain
farm in Alberta, Canada, where his father had settled after coming from
the Ukraine. Then the family moved to a dairy farm in Manitoba, not
far from the United States border, which is the setting of this book.

Later, when William Kurelek was sixteen, he was sent to high school
in the city, where he was eager to tell his new friends about his adventures living close to nature. No one seemed interested in listening
and it was many years before Kurelek found a way to hold an audience —
through his pictures.

William Kurelek's paintings are represented in major art museums
in Canada, the United States, and England.

3